Doctor, Doctor

Mary Rose

T0347650

Name _____

Age _____

Class _____

OXFORD
UNIVERSITY PRESS

OXFORD
UNIVERSITY PRESS

Great Clarendon Street, Oxford OX2 6DP

Oxford University Press is a department of the University of Oxford.
It furthers the University's objective of excellence in research, scholarship,
and education by publishing worldwide in

Oxford New York

Auckland Cape Town Dar es Salaam Hong Kong Karachi
Kuala Lumpur Madrid Melbourne Mexico City Nairobi
New Delhi Shanghai Taipei Toronto

With offices in

Argentina Austria Brazil Chile Czech Republic France Greece
Guatemala Hungary Italy Japan Poland Portugal Singapore
South Korea Switzerland Thailand Turkey Ukraine Vietnam

OXFORD and OXFORD ENGLISH are registered trade marks of
Oxford University Press in the UK and in certain other countries

© Oxford University Press 2005

The moral rights of the author have been asserted

Database right Oxford University Press (maker)

First published 2005

2022

23

No unauthorized photocopying

All rights reserved. No part of this publication may be reproduced,
stored in a retrieval system, or transmitted, in any form or by any means,
without the prior permission in writing of Oxford University Press,
or as expressly permitted by law, or under terms agreed with the appropriate
reprographics rights organization. Enquiries concerning reproduction
outside the scope of the above should be sent to the ELT Rights Department,
Oxford University Press, at the address above

You must not circulate this book in any other binding or cover
and you must impose this same condition on any acquirer

Any websites referred to in this publication are in the public domain and
their addresses are provided by Oxford University Press for information only.
Oxford University Press disclaims any responsibility for the content

ISBN: 978 0 19 440075 6

Printed in China

ACKNOWLEDGEMENTS

Illustrations by: Arlene Adams

With thanks to Sally Spray for her contribution to this series

Reading Dolphins
Notes for teachers & parents

📖 Using the book

1 Begin by looking at the first story page (page 2). Look at the picture and ask questions about it. Then read the story text under the picture with your students. **Use section 1 of the CD for this if possible.**

2 Teach and check the understanding of any new vocabulary. Note that some of the words are in the **Picture Dictionary** at the back of the book.

3 Now look at the activities on the right-hand page. Show the example to the students and instruct them to complete the activities. This may be done individually, in pairs, or as a class.

4 Do the same for the remaining pages of the book.

5 Retell the whole story more quickly, reinforcing the new vocabulary. **Sections 2 and 3 of the CD can help with this.**

6 **If possible, listen to the expanded story (section 4 of the CD). The students should follow in their books.**

7 When the book is finished, use the **Picture Dictionary** to check that students understand and remember new vocabulary. **Section 5 of the CD can help with this.**

💿 Using the CD

The CD contains five sections.

1 The story told slowly, with pauses. Use this during the first reading. It may also be used for "Listen and repeat" activities at any point.

2 The story told at normal speed. This should be used once the students have read the book for the first time.

3 The story chanted. Students may want to chant along with the story.

4 The expanded story. The story is told in a longer version. This will help the students understand English when it is spoken faster, as they will now know the story and the vocabulary.

5 Vocabulary. Each word in the **Picture Dictionary** is spoken and then used in a simple sentence.

Connect.

flower •

tree •

foot •

head •

hand •

girl •

Connect.

My head hurts.

My foot hurts.

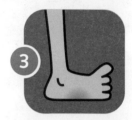

My hand hurts.

My knee hurts.

My ear hurts.

My finger hurts.

6

Circle yes or no .

1. Her hand hurts.   yes   (no)

2. Her head hurts.   yes   no

3. Her foot hurts.   yes   no

4. Her knee hurts.   yes   no

5. I can see three children.   yes   no

6. I can see two chairs.   yes   no

7. I can see two blue chairs.   yes   no

8. I can see four red chairs.   yes   no

Number.

black 2 yellow ☐

blue ☐ red ☐

white ☐ pink ☐

Number.

door [2]   head [ ]

window [ ]   chair [ ]

floor [ ]   doctor [ ]

Circle yes or no .

1. Katy is six.   yes no

2. Katy is a boy.   yes no

3. Katy is a girl.   yes no

4. Katy's head hurts. yes no

5. Katy is in a tree.   yes no

6. Katy is on a chair. yes no

7. Katy is at school.   yes no

8. Katy is with Doctor Green. yes no

Connect.

chair •

head •

foot •

tree •

door •

hand •

knee •

window •

Picture Dictionary

black

ear

blue

finger

chair

flower

door

foot

hand

tree

head

white

knee

window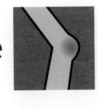

pink

yellow

red

Dolphin Readers

Dolphin Readers are available at five levels, from Starter to 4.

The Dolphins series covers four major themes:

Grammar, Living Together, The World Around Us, Science and Nature.

For each theme, there are two titles at every level.

Activity Books are available for all Dolphins.

All Dolphins are available on audio CD.
(2 TITLES ON EACH CD ⌀ SEE TABLE BELOW)

Teacher's Notes are available at **www.oup.com/elt/dolphins**

	Grammar	Living Together	The World Around Us	Science and Nature
Starter	•Silly Squirrel •Monkeying Around	•My Family •A Day with Baby	•Doctor, Doctor •Moving House	•A Game of Shapes •Baby Animals
Level 1	•Meet Molly •Where Is It?	•Little Helpers •Jack the Hero	•On Safari •Lost Kitten	•Number Magic •How's the Weather?
Level 2	•Double Trouble •Super Sam	•Candy for Breakfast •Lost!	•A Visit to the City •Matt's Mistake	•Numbers, Numbers Everywhere •Circles and Squares
Level 3	•Students in Space •What Did You Do Yesterday?	•New Girl in School •Uncle Jerry's Great Idea	•Just Like Mine •Wonderful Wild Animals	•Things That Fly •Let's Go to the Rainforest
Level 4	•The Tough Task •Yesterday, Today and Tomorrow	•We Won the Cup •Up and Down	•Where People Live •City Girl, Country Boy	•In the Ocean •Go, Gorillas, Go